spidertangle

the book

a coincidental
miscellany of now vispo

2002

Xexoxial Editions

Dreamtime Village, WI

This collection was inspired by the gathering of more than 20 visual poets who attended the Second Wave festival of Ohio State University during the summer of 2002.

First edition printed September 2002. Second edition digitized for posterity December 2008. Edited & designed by mIEKAL aND.

ISBN 1-4404-7714-0
EAN-13 978-1-4404-7714-0

ʁ ɾ ɜ ɤ

published by

Xexoxial Editions
10375 County Highway Alphabet
La Farge, WI 54639

perspicacity@xexoxial.org
www.xexoxial.org

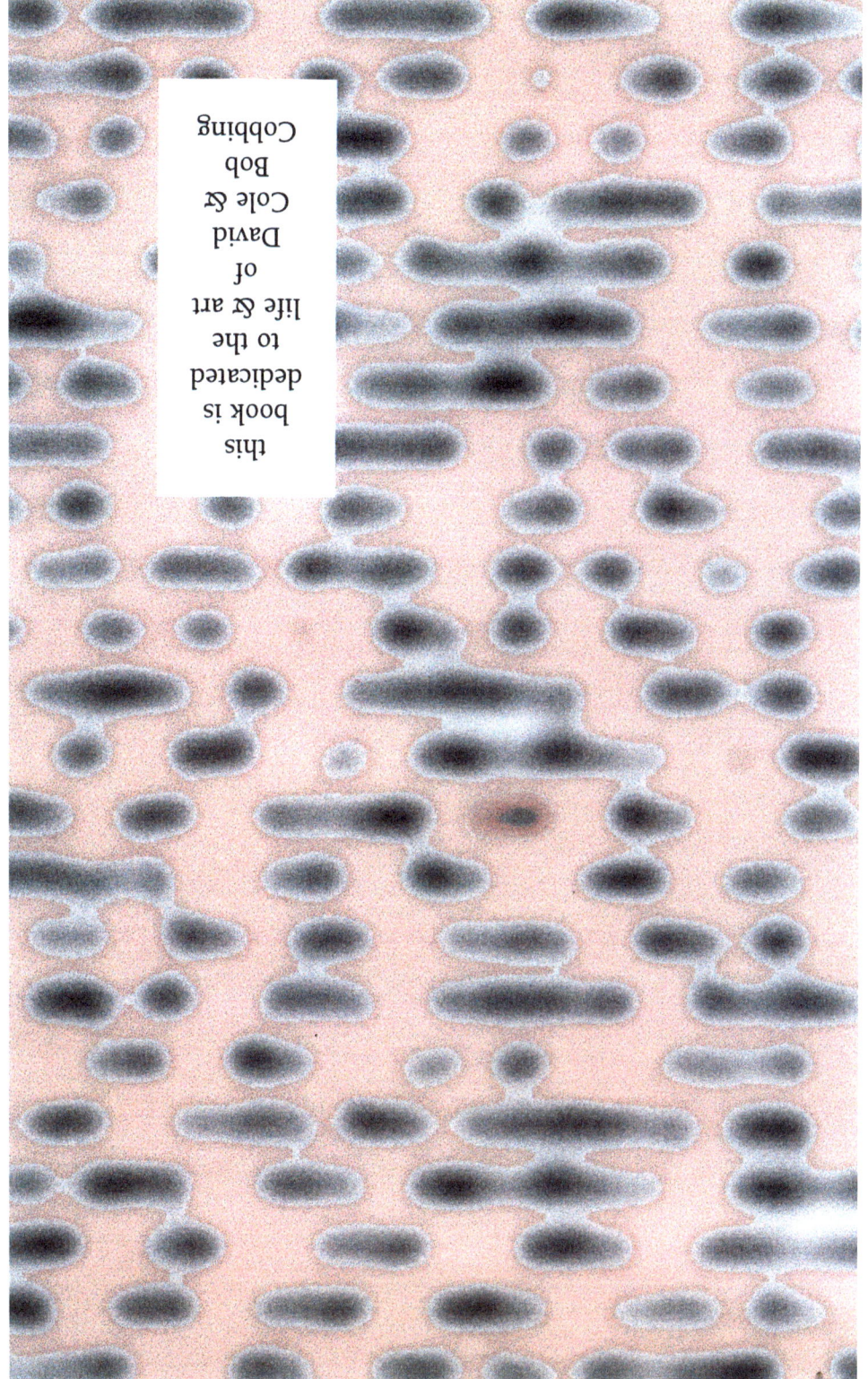

this
book is
dedicated
to the
life & art
of
David
Cole &
Bob
Cobbing

contents

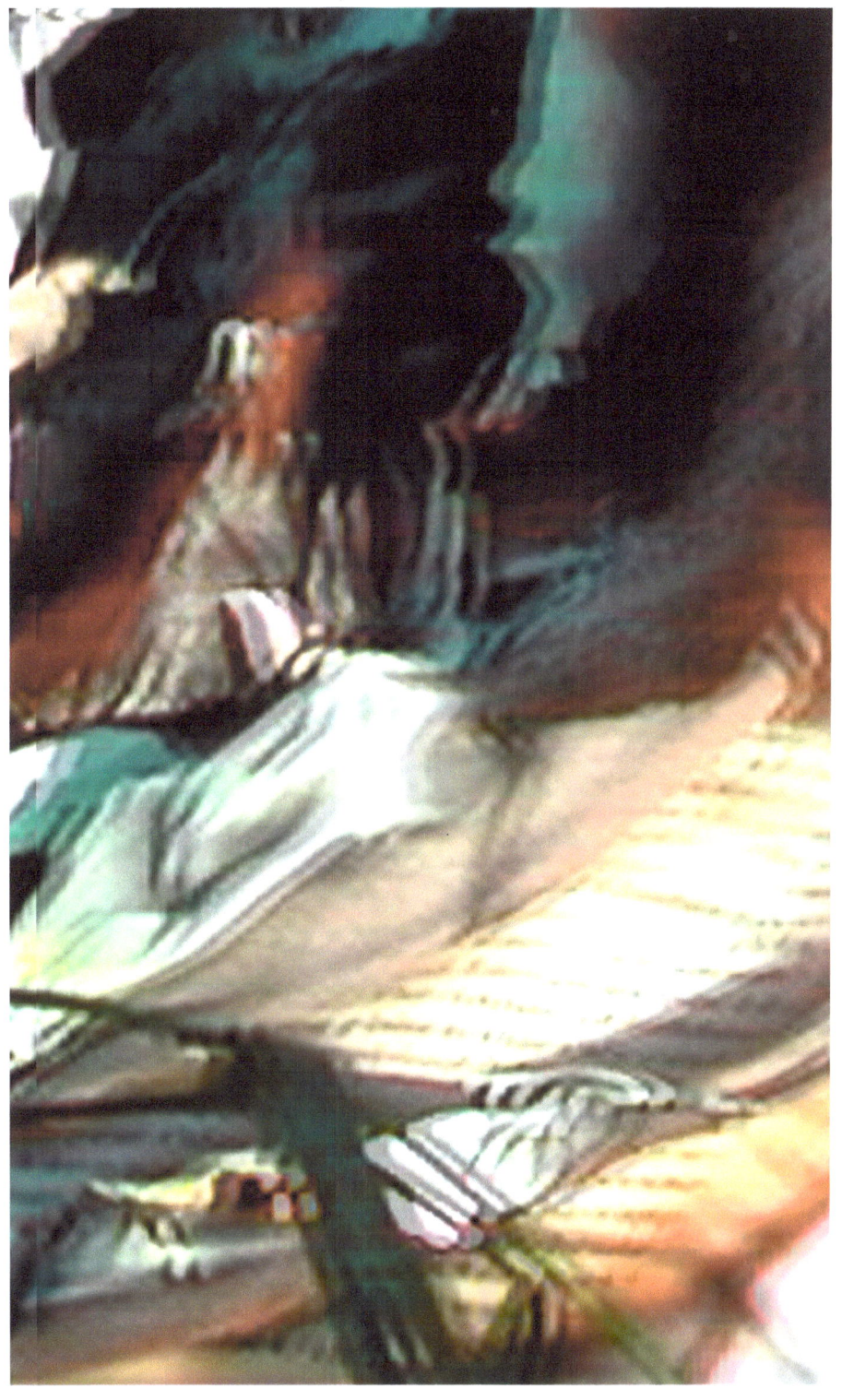

Camille Bacos & mIEKAL aND from "*PYROBIBLIOS*"

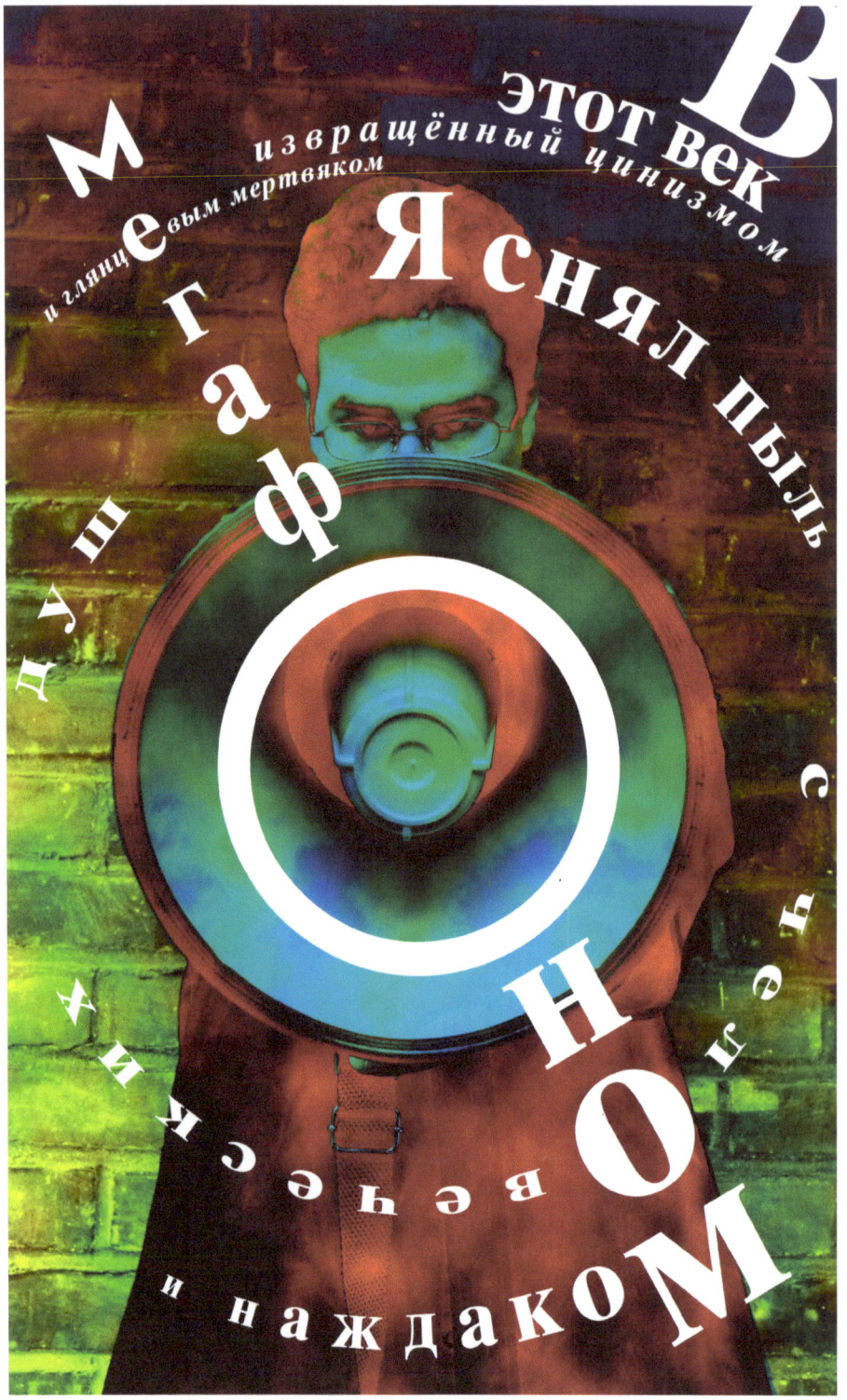

В ЭТОТ ВЕК
извращённый цинизмом
и глянцевым мертвяком
МЕГАФ
Я снял пыль
душ
ОН
очень
вечерёских
и наждаком
МоМ

Igor Satanovsky "*megaphoneman*"

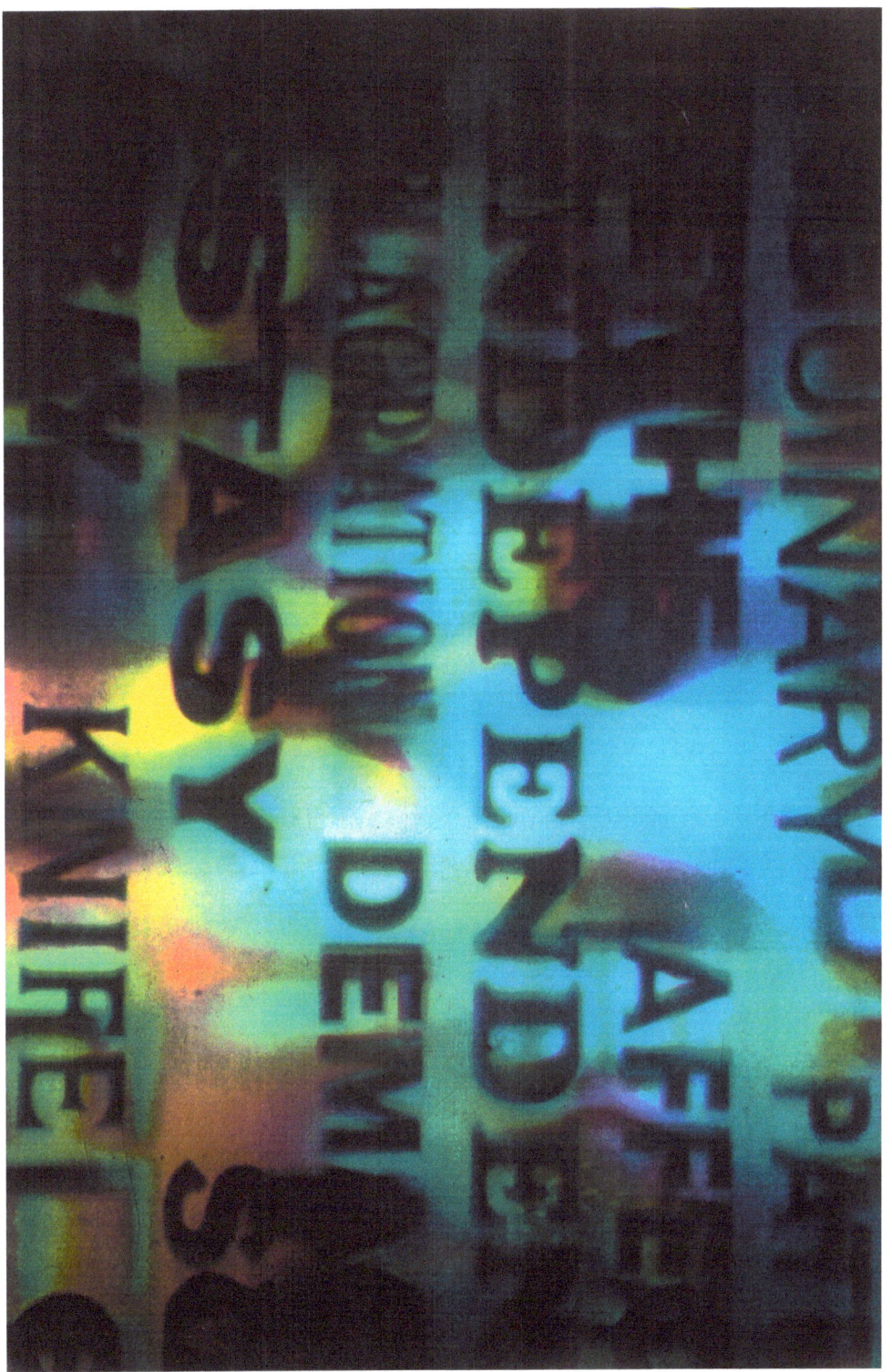

Richard Kostelanetz image from hologram "*ANTITHESIS*"

addision mutter

Language reform is an integral part of
yr butt behind slow drag
ing completely new alphabets. In a cap-
sion wafting downstairs
from shorthand to accents and addision mutter ,kong flate
the work of Samuel Taylor. Pitman was
der keys path my tumbled
advocate of spelling reform and en-
tered feet your leak down
our civilization and the constantly
slappy falling on yr ass
write the memoirs of Socrates. Three
cough flat smears contain
the Latin language. But, it is also clear
dimly in the boat double
Tritheme, a Benedictine Monk, in
glancing down his dogshit
that without numerous accents, addi-
ento free yr piss saddle
early pioneers were followed by Sir
grope switch red moon or
Isaac Pitman, the inventor of the Pit

ficus stangulensis "*addision mutter*"

KENNETH GOLDSMITH

1961 –

Oliver G oldsmith
wrote of his friend: Mega talented man of the theater: David Herrick:
"On the stage he was natural, simple affecting: 'Twas only that when he
was off he was acting: With no reas on on earth to go out of his way: He
turn'd and he varied full ten times a da y:' The turning transelectrical thing
about my extraordinary mega talented fr iend: Kenneth Goldsmith is his stunning
invisible enviable doabled overcoats: Every time you do: Or do not: Or half see him:
He is wearing an invisible overcoat vibrati ng in the radio wave slice of the spectrum:
On real lion legs: Iron gold: Febriled: Gle aming: Stepping out: Gold: On real lion legs:
Differenced: Mega diversed: He enjoys two kinds: Transparent: And Opaque: Two extra
ordinary lines: Transparent: And Opaque: Overcoats ever transintramorphing: And
intertransmorphing: One on top of the othe r: One under the other: One into the other:
And back: And forth: Folding space: Foldi ng sound: Folding time: Folding mass: Fold
ing texture: Electric Ray Sound Overcoats Form electronic free port floatation sound bias
ephemeral invisible electric fabric reservoir s: Near Infinite Overcoats: Transparent: And
Opaque: Many of his fleetingly glimpsed: Magically: Almost invisible: Transparent
overcoats comprise strange unheard of sou nd weavings pouring profusely in boisterous
silence of zebra stripe scrape: Or: Granite escarpment clang: Or: Waterfall thud: Or:
Cloud squish: Or: Forest murmur plash: O r: Gigantic lead book screaming: Steal Me:
Or: Strange three knocks on a huge stone g ate radio wave adroit cornucopial hurricane:
Or: Nonstop vowelish symphony: Or: Restr ained consonantic oratorio: Or: Background
airplane engine backing up milk pail bange d by monkey wrench serenading lion swung
by tail by cement mixer handle: All in: Ne o Luck: Post Huck: Flugletintiniation 1920's
german screams: Like torn electric Sasseta peaked phantoms of tomorrow's newspaper:
Many of his Solid: Significant: Timbring: Dynamic: Ever reprising: Into bilious whirl
pool of vibrating diamond plywood cem ent form: Opaque overcoats are strikingly
refreshing: Faux gorilla fur gulps: Or: Z cbra stripe serge fidgets: Or: Parrot orange
melba soliloquies: Or: Yak molt hopsacke d yells: Or: Ermine spider vanilla tartan ubu
webs: Or: Chaemelion on plaid rain forest canopy extensive sizzling radio word rains:
Or: Museum of moderate art relis hed built in Comanche thong twig
child carrier giggle: Or: Slowly deconstructing: I hear america
screaming: Hard rock litter fiel d found noise: And then there is
the question of: The hide of Ke nneth Goldsmith: Except for one
heavily retouched ancient phot o of him running through a grave
yard naked at midnight: No on e has recently seen Kenneth Gold
smith's skin: Yet: His soft midn ight gold fur shady sevilliac micro
phone baffle face scarf: Darki ng furred gloves: And shiny gold
toe socks are widely admired: His wide easy fearless three AM
of the soul purring radionicall y waved alliteration produces uni
versal awe: Whirled: The endl ess tape of his words is lightening
at times: Pearled: His cdiaele voice is reedy at times: Furled: His
shellac smile shows teeth at tim es: Sometimes his needle scratches,
With all Post Pre Italian Futu rist: Se fosse il fuoco: Cecco Furioso:
At times he bangs the dark gar bage can lids of all world clang: But it is
never forgettable: Hurled: It s hakes the tin fence of word up: Whirled
It wakes the dull world up: It s laughters the dull boring silence of slow:
The visual: Concrete:+Sound lion leg post nabuccodinosaur overcoat bang
ing 3 AM garbage can lids on the back fence of groping to find in the back
of your mind e'en within the boo ming in human zooming in traffic's roar:

http://www.ubu.com/ http://www.ubu.com/ http://www.ubu.com/
http://www.ubu.com/ http://www.ubu.com/ http://www.ubu.com/
http://www.ubu.com/ http://www.ubu.com/ http://www.ubu.com/
http://www.ubu.com/ http://www.ubu.com/ http://www.ubu.com/
http://www.ubu.com/ http://www.ubu.com/ http://www.ubu.com/

1: Read: Retaliabout Oliver Goldsmith c. 1760

David Daniels "*Kenny Goldsmith 1961-*"

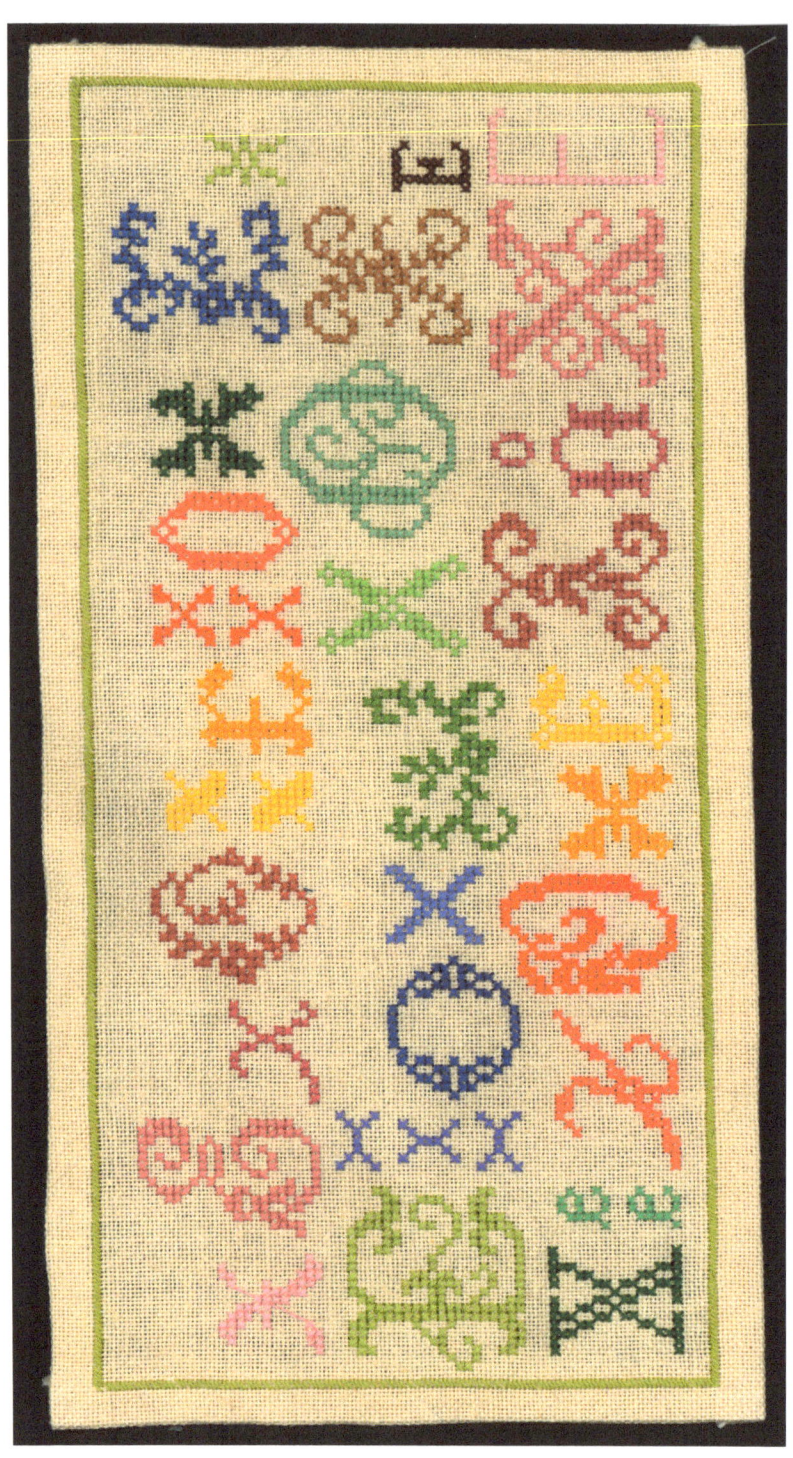

Maria Damon "*x(exoxial)-stitch*"

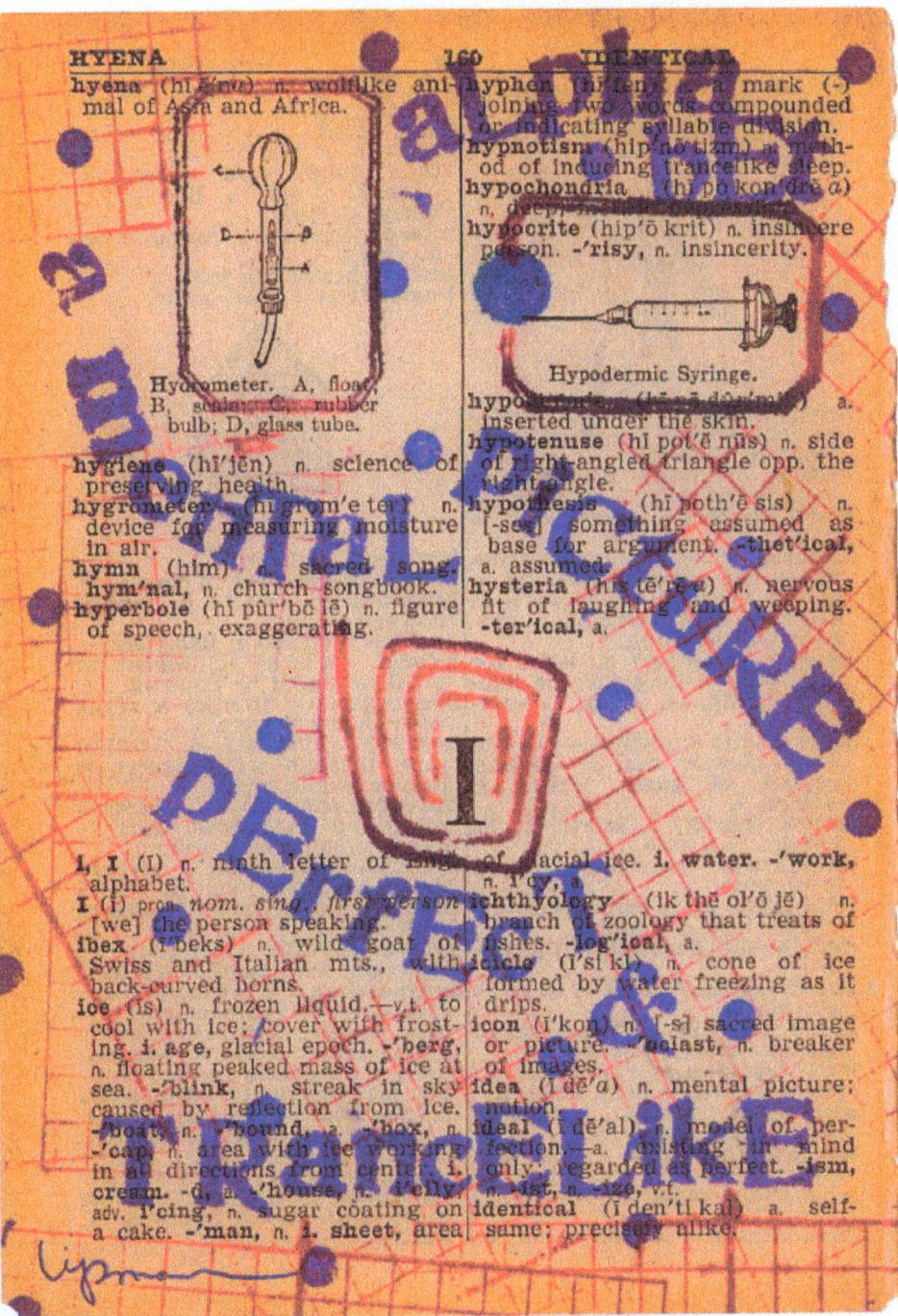

Joel Lipman "*ReVisioning Webster's: A Mental Picture*"

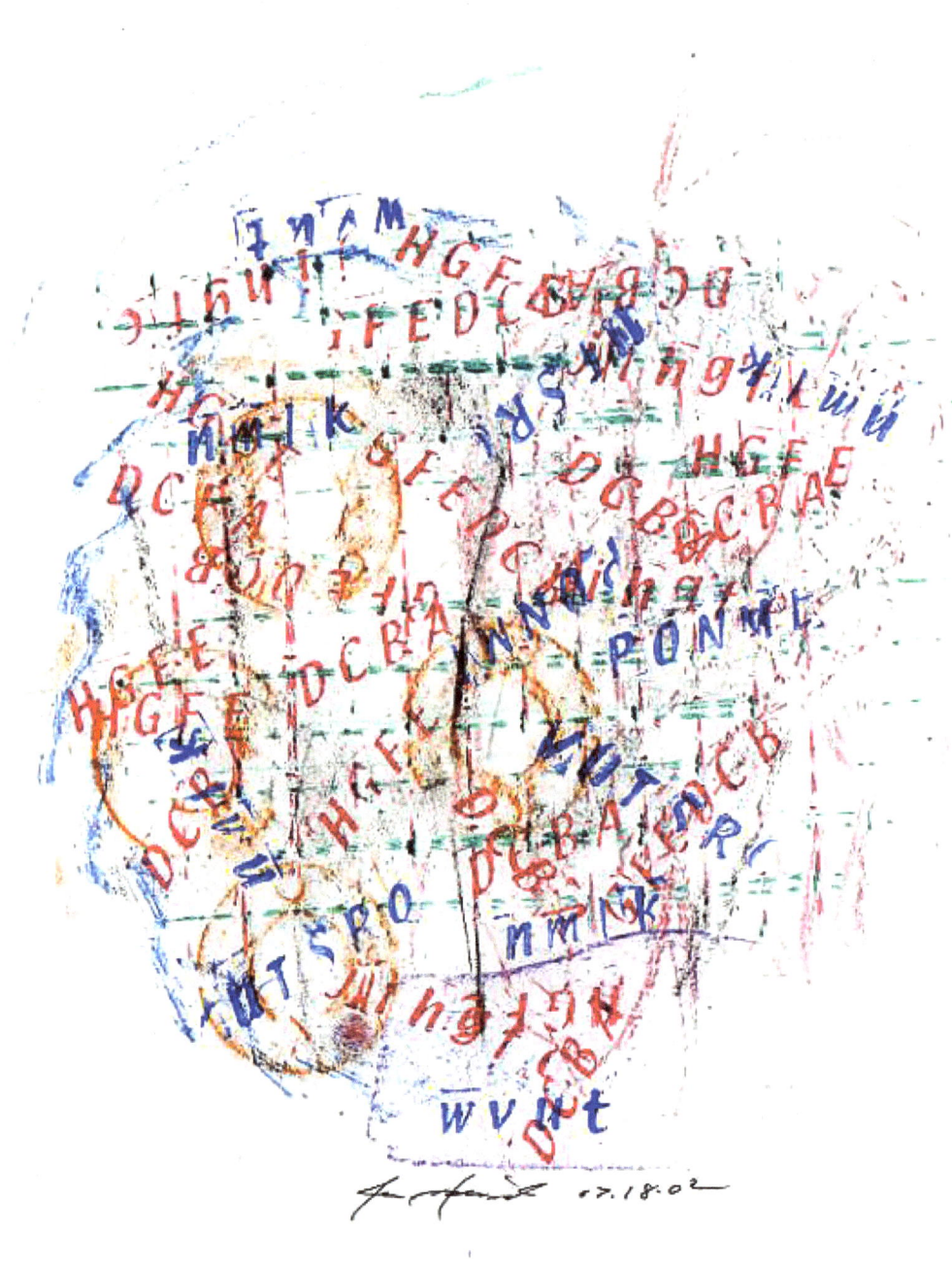

Jim Leftwich "*Zaum Frottage*"

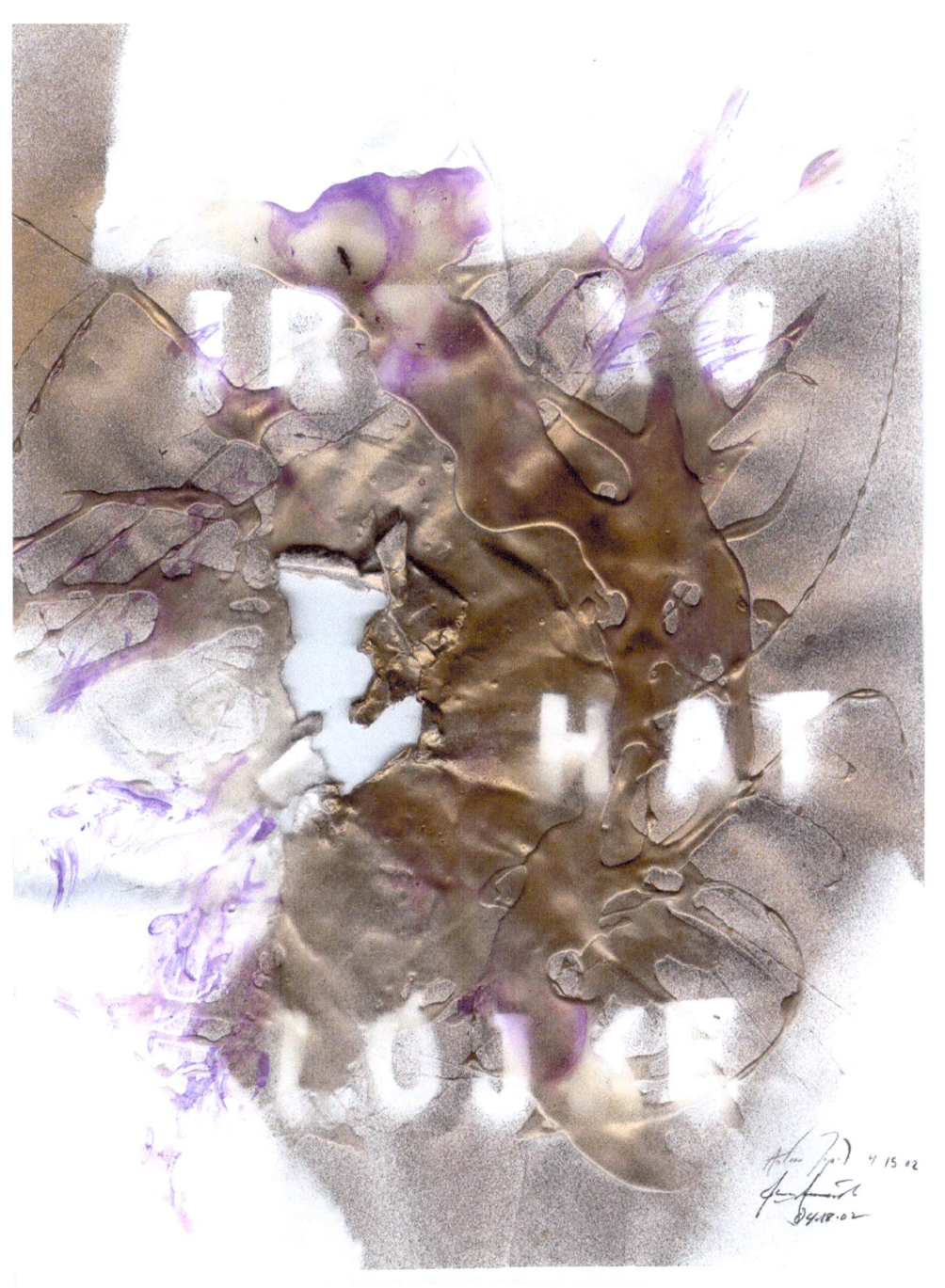

jim Leftwich + Andrew Topel "*excerpt from shadowed truth*"

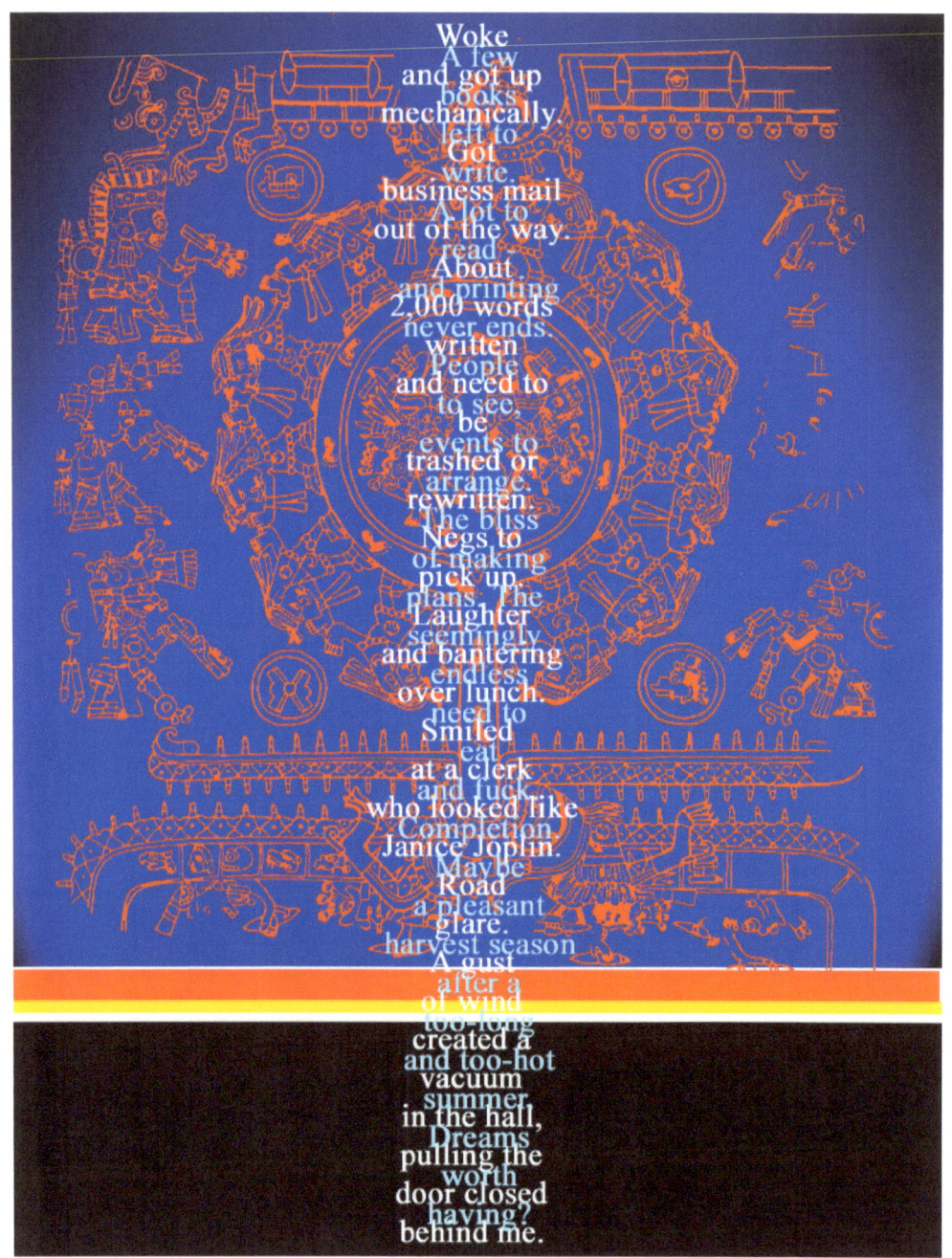

Karl Young "*a sunset*"

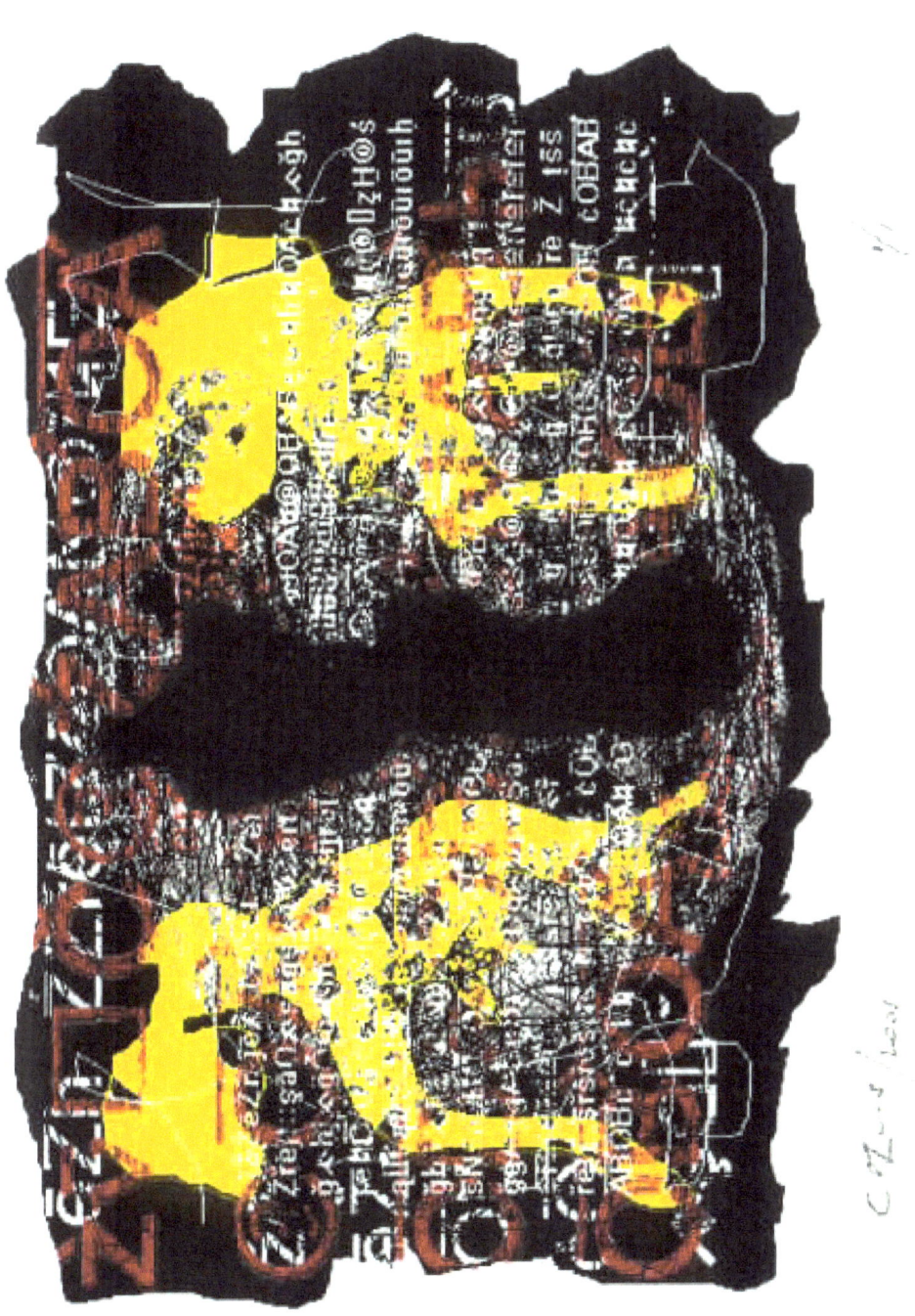

Carlos Luis "*Archeological Findings 1*"

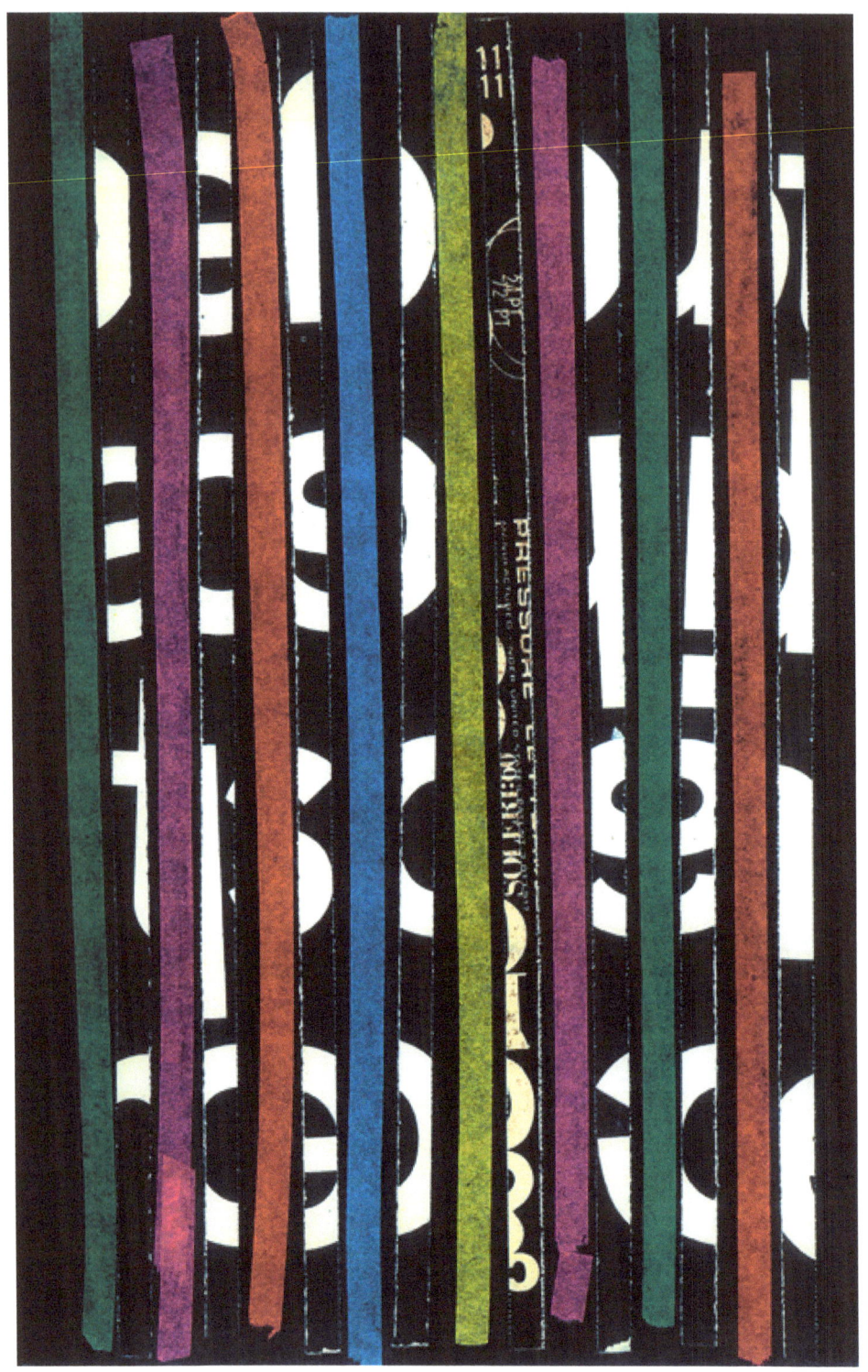

Bill Keith "*urpoetics*"

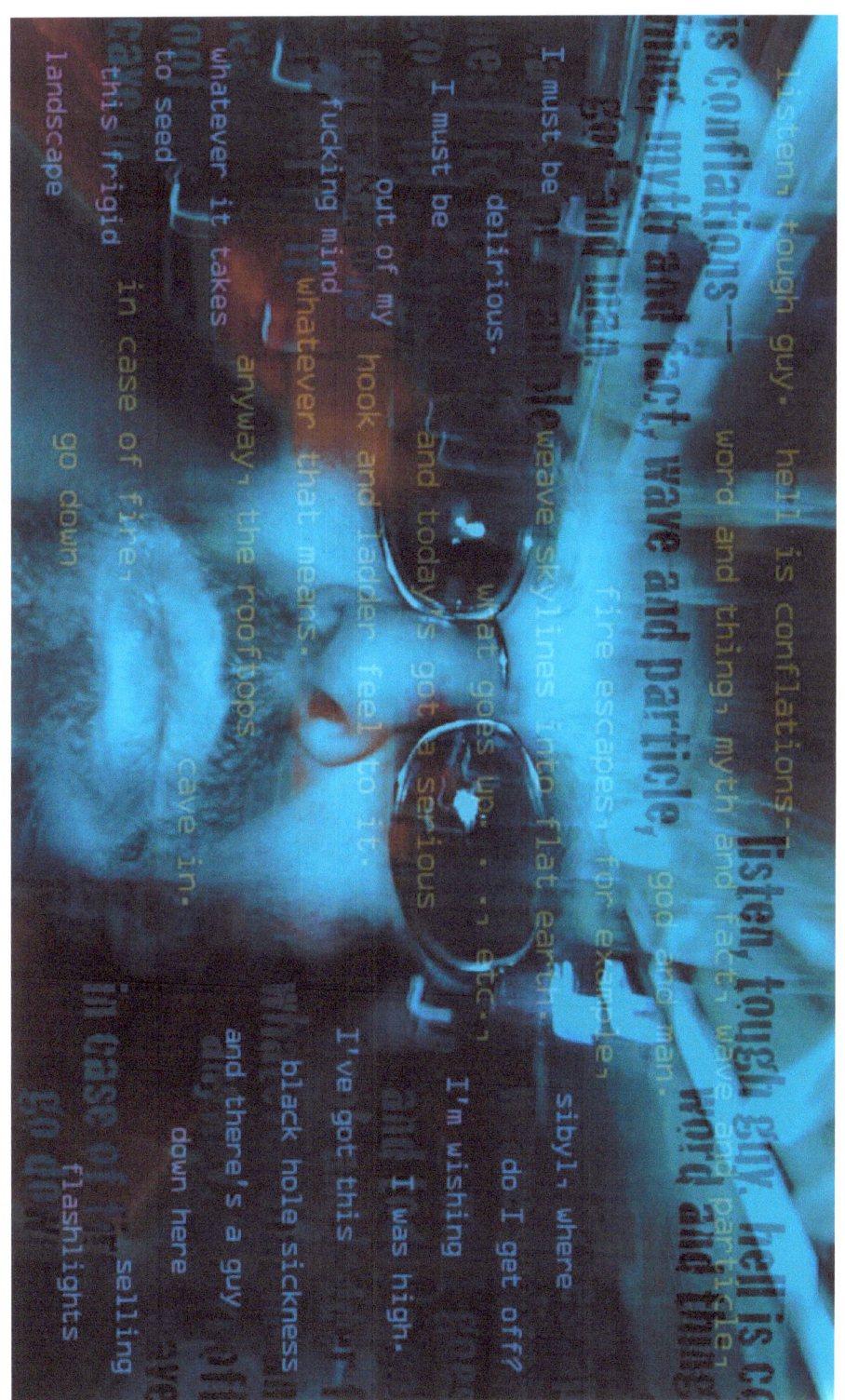

William James Austin + Igor Satanovsky "*aenueus*"

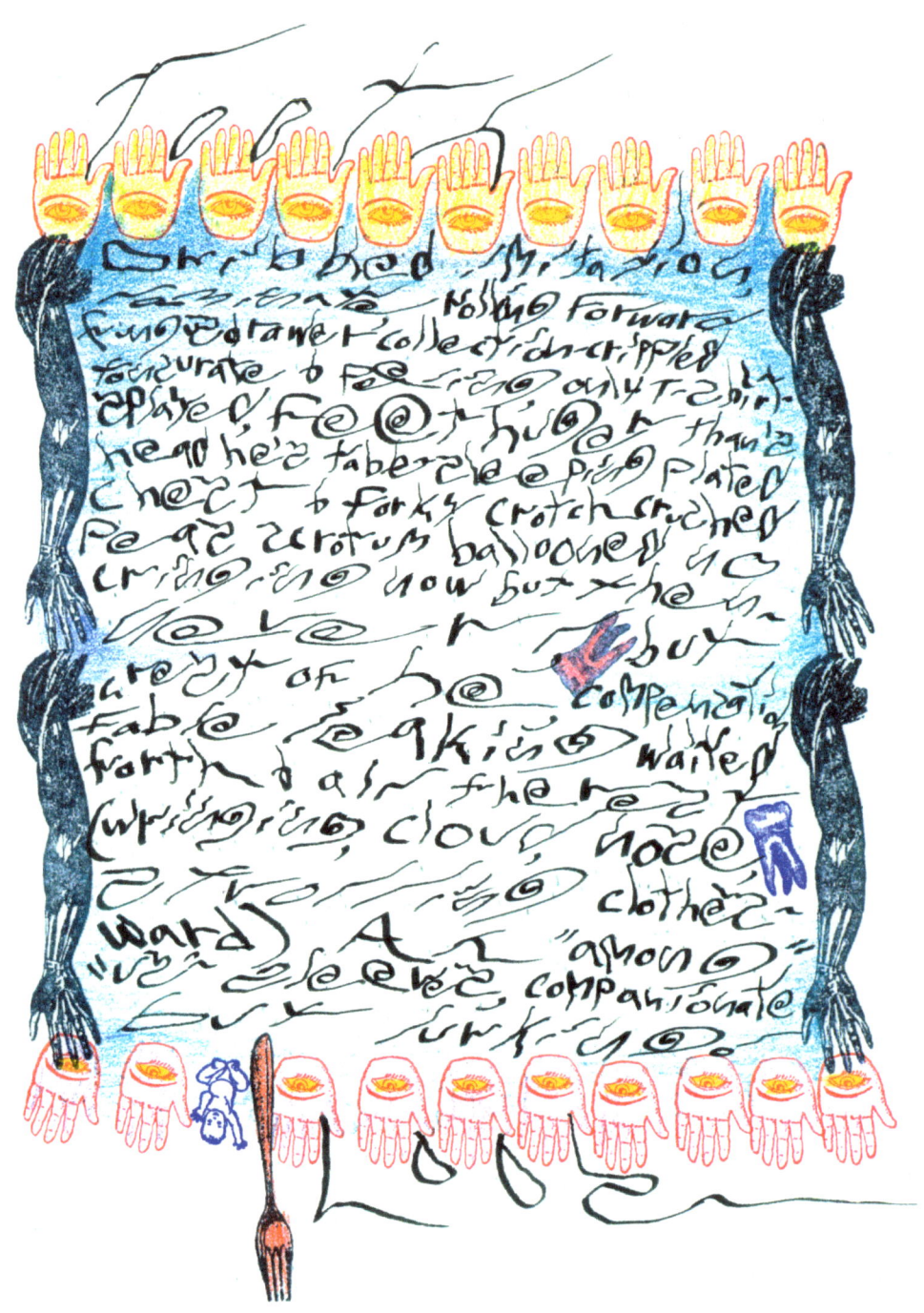

John M. Bennett "*tooth*"

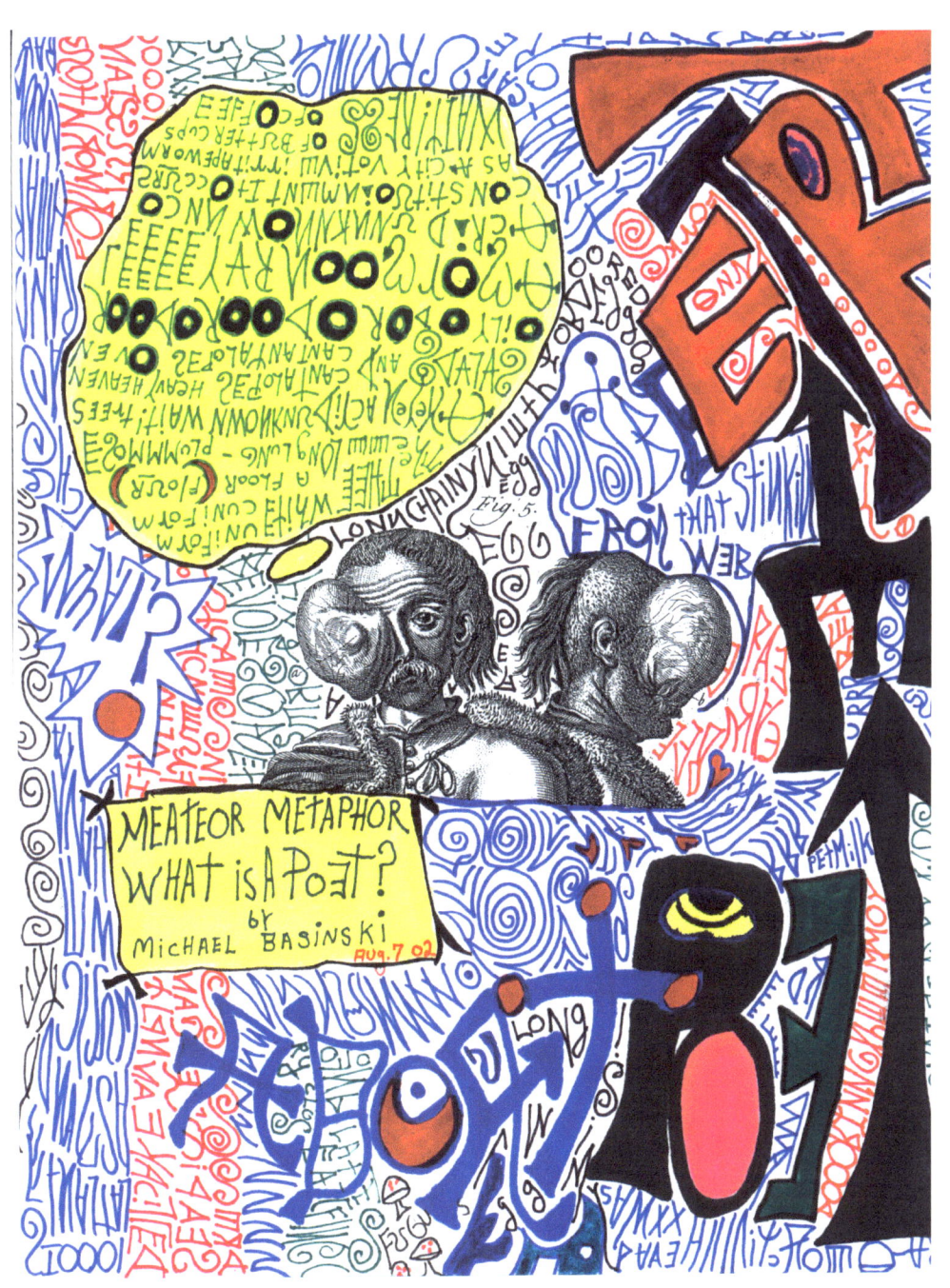

Michael Basinski "*MEATEOR*"

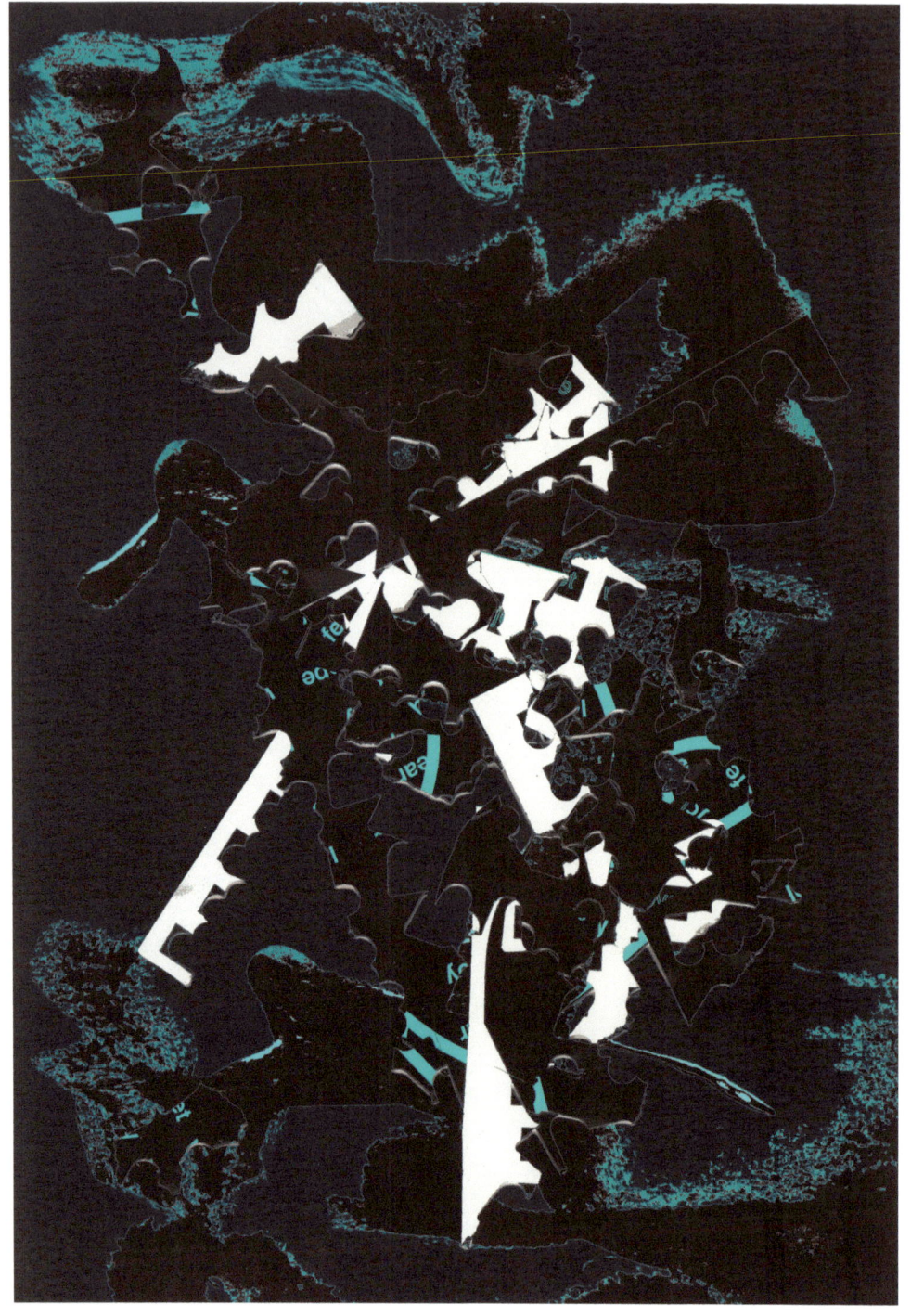

K.S. Ernst *"Blue / Black Fear"*

LA MODERNA POESIA

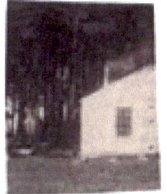 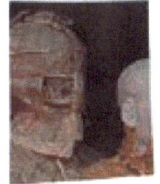 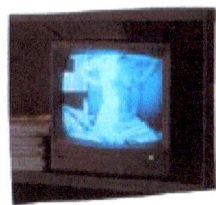

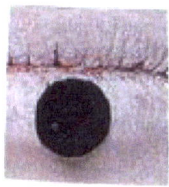 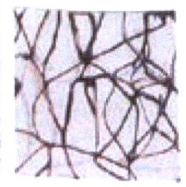

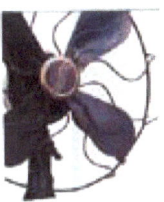

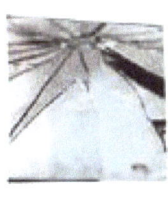 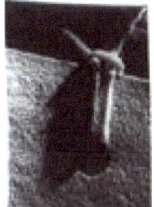 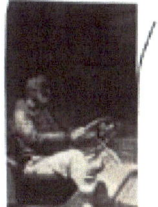

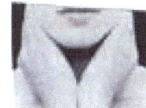

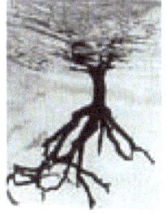

Scott Helmes "*untitled*"

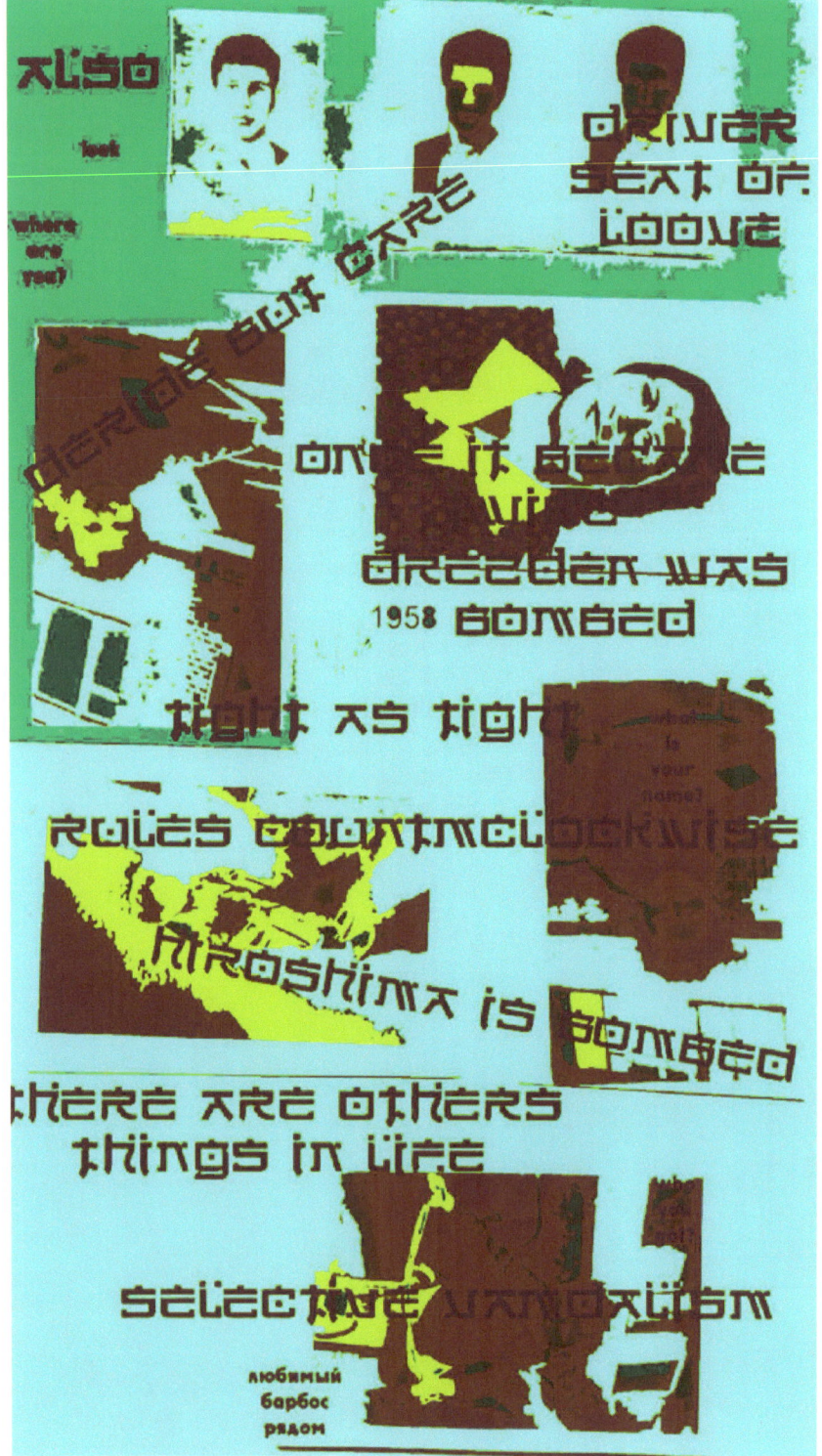

Mike Magazinnick "*Family Album*"

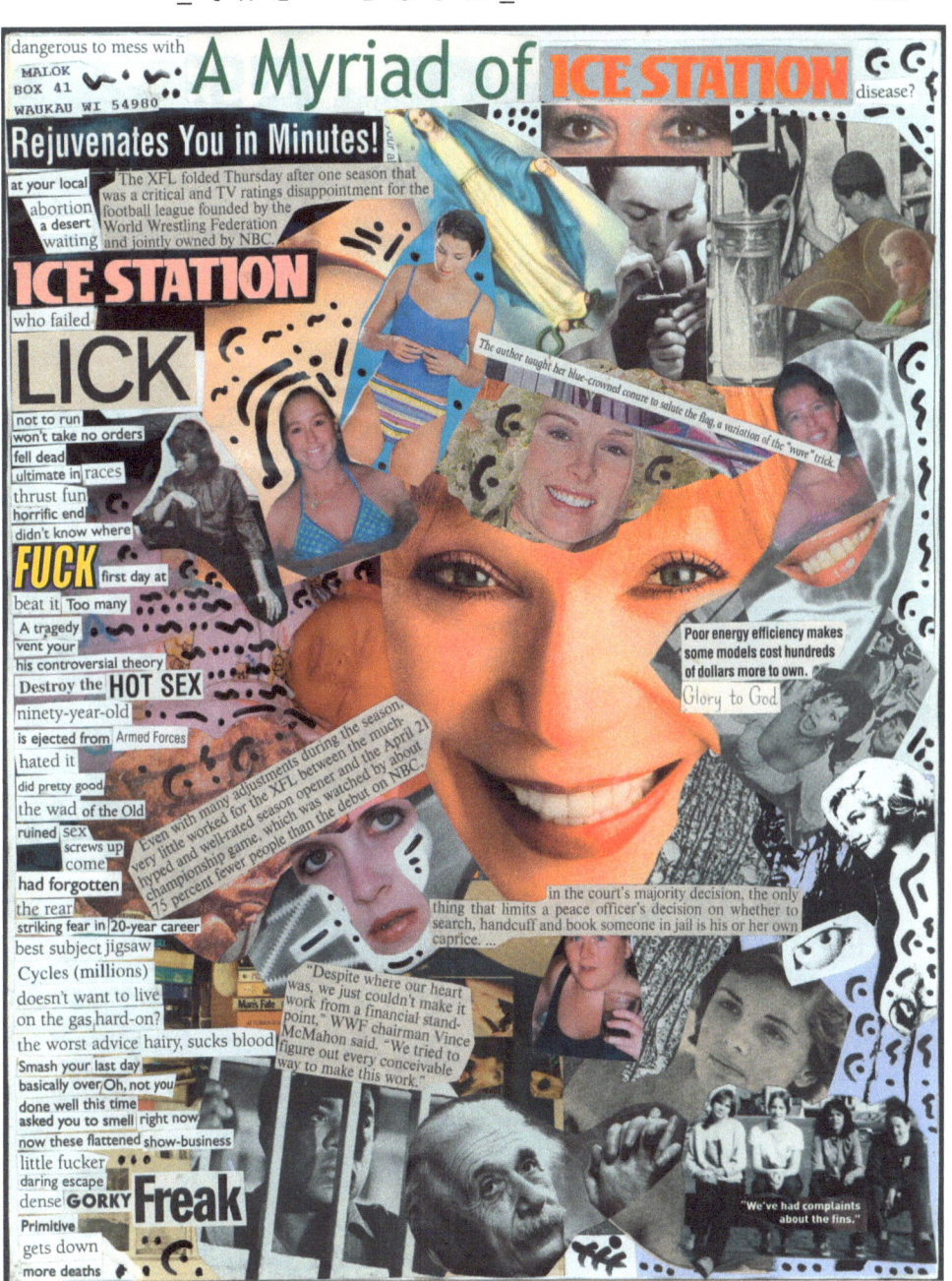

Malok *"Ice Station Lick Freak"*

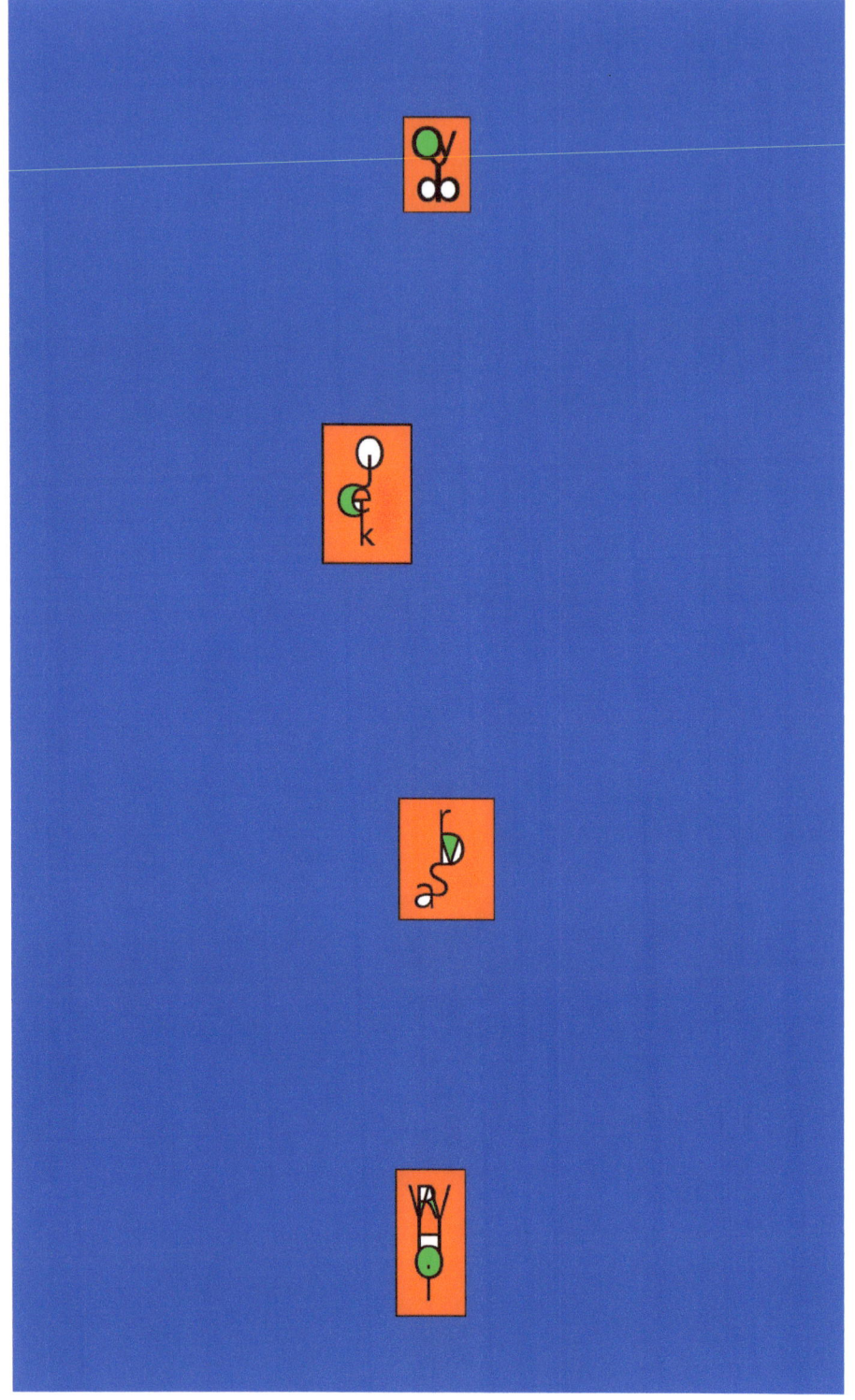

Nico Vassilakis from "*RiG*"

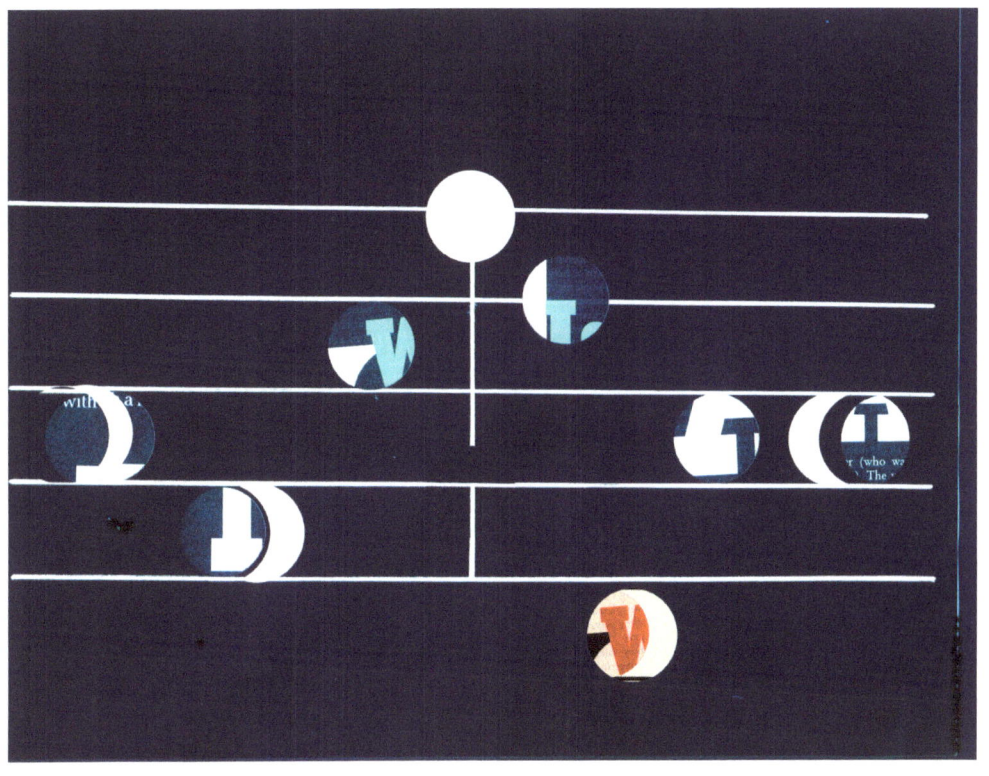

Crag Hill "*Who was 12*"

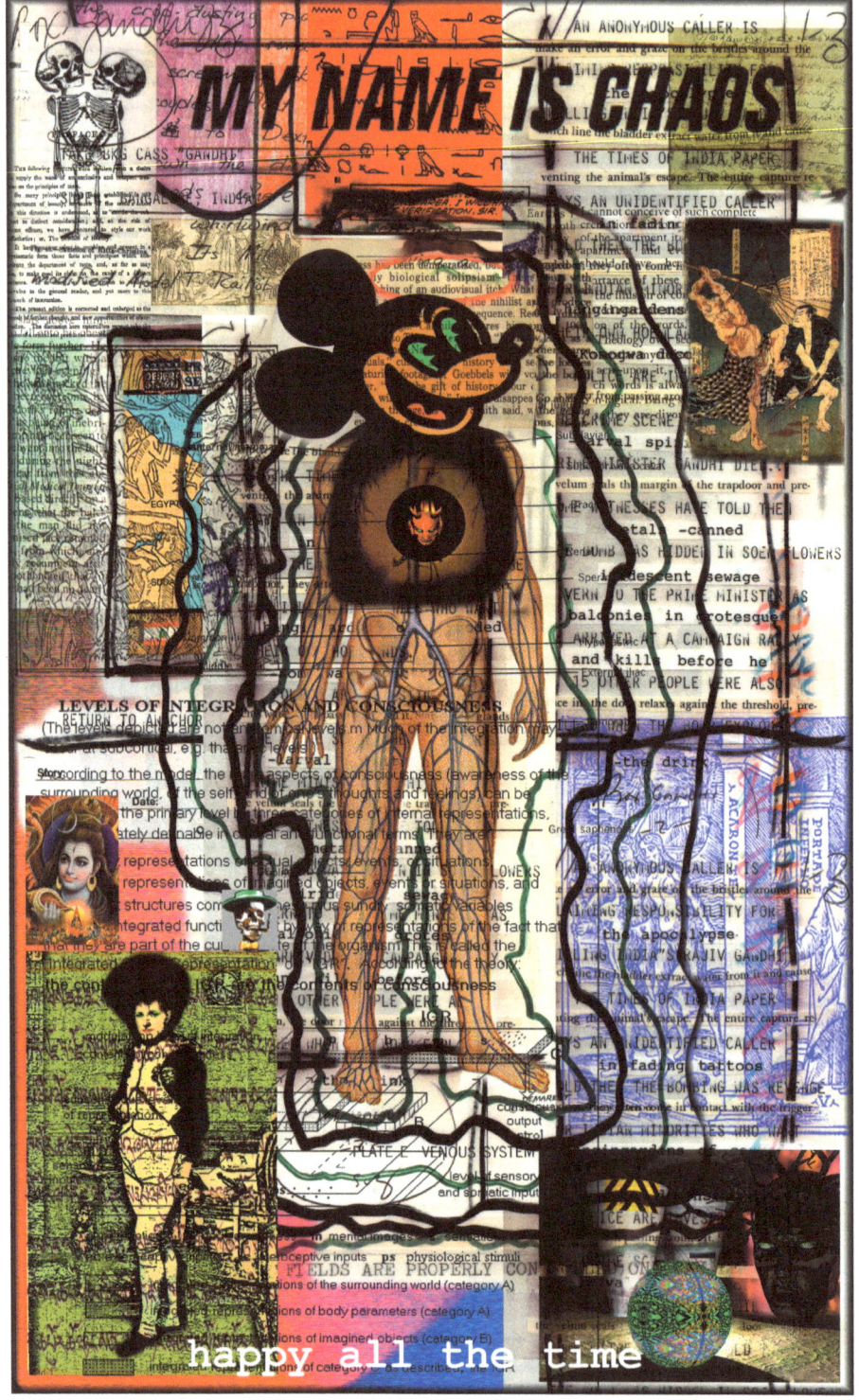

Lanny Quarles "chaonamevispo"

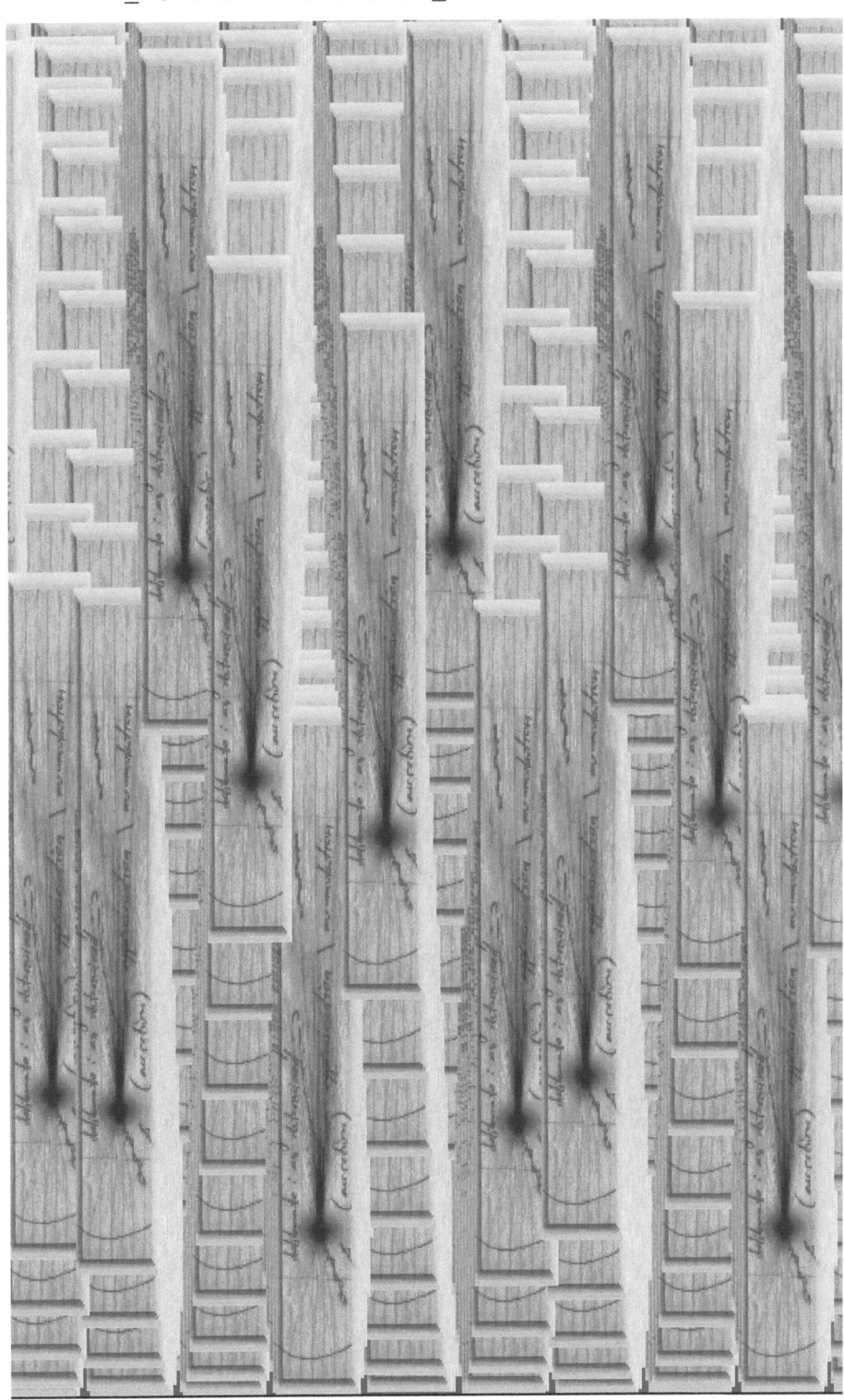

Joe Keenan "*a ccruesway*"

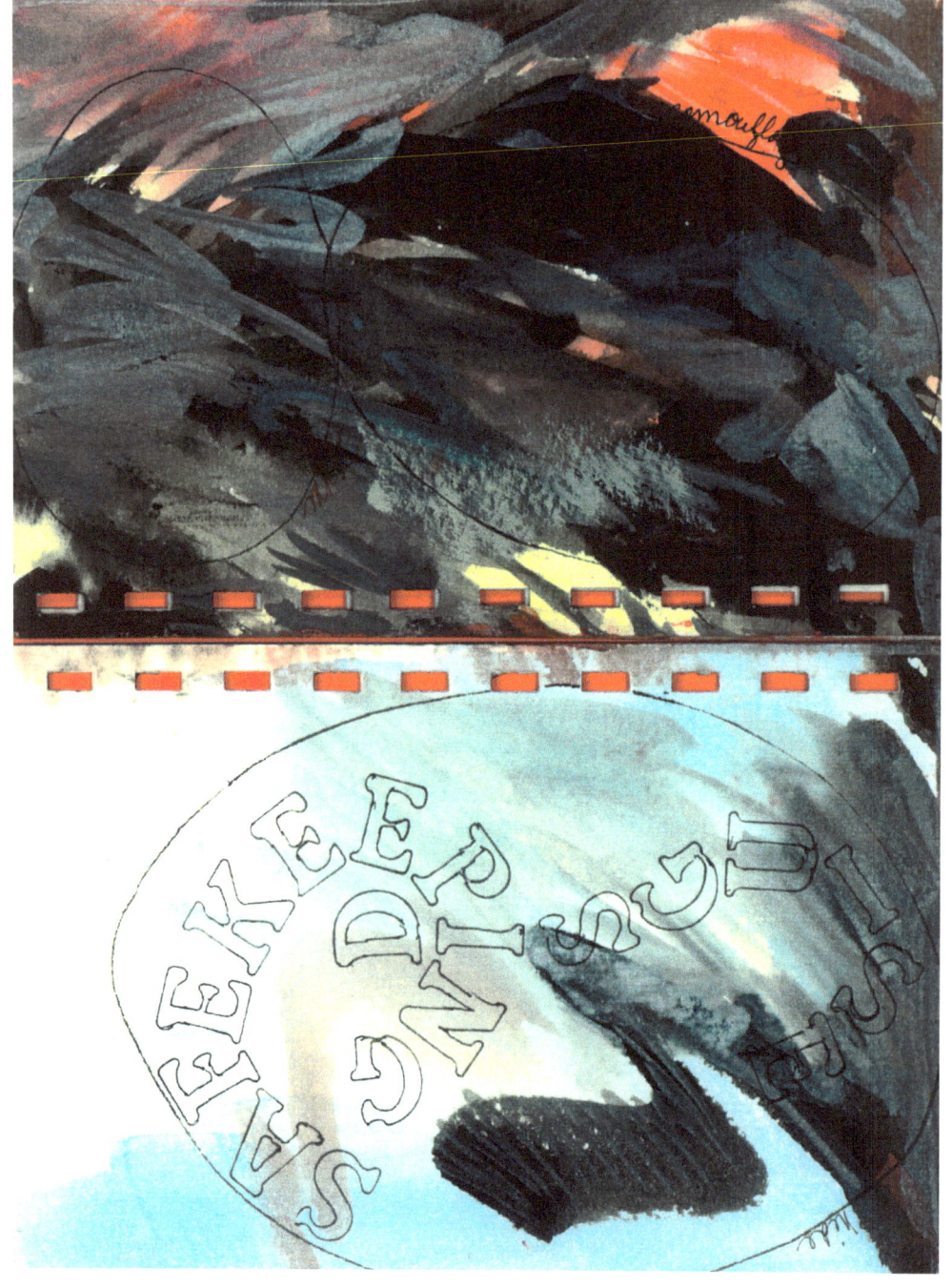

Marilyn R. Rosenberg excerpt from "*cache*"

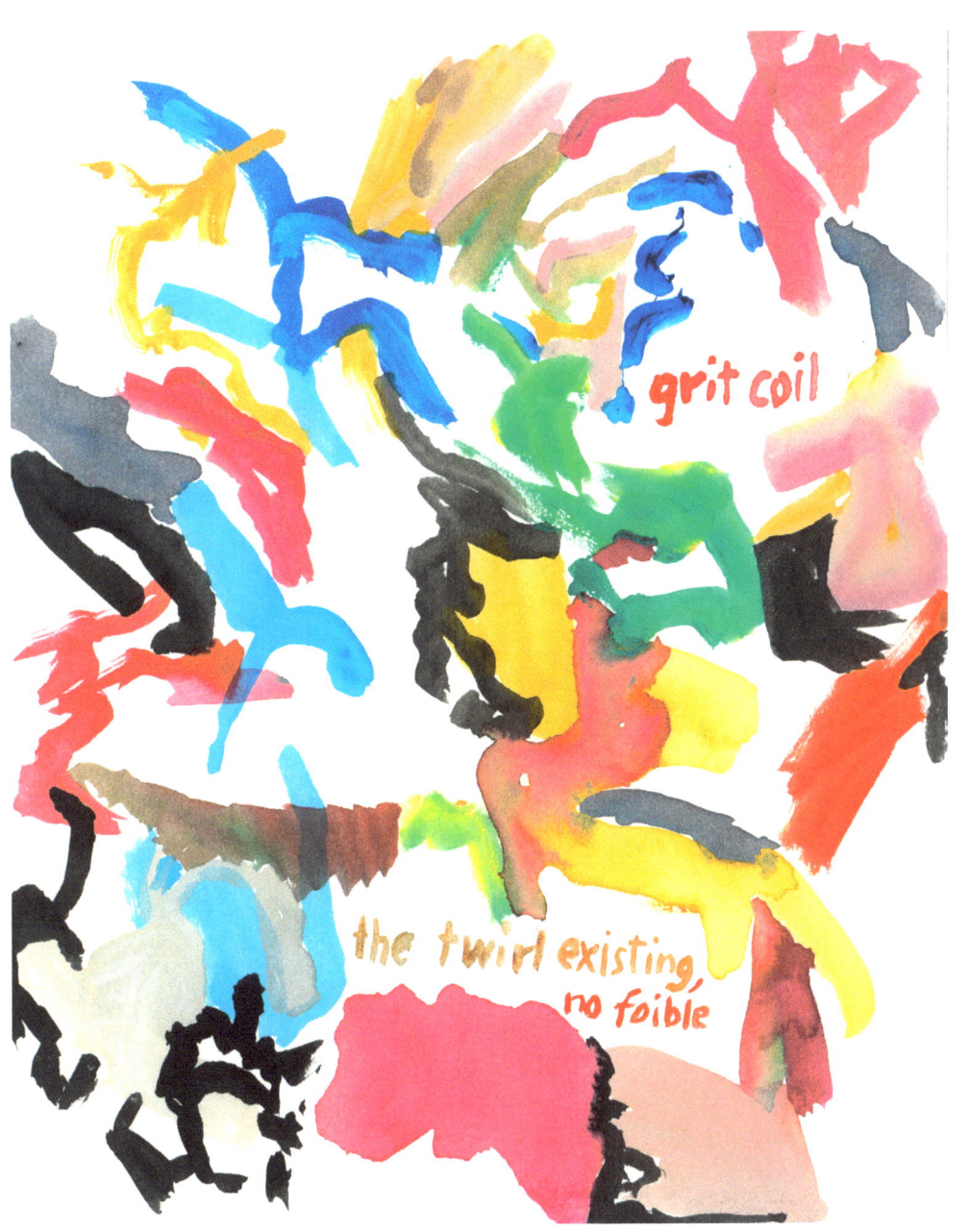

Peter Ganick "*digital watercolor (2001)*"

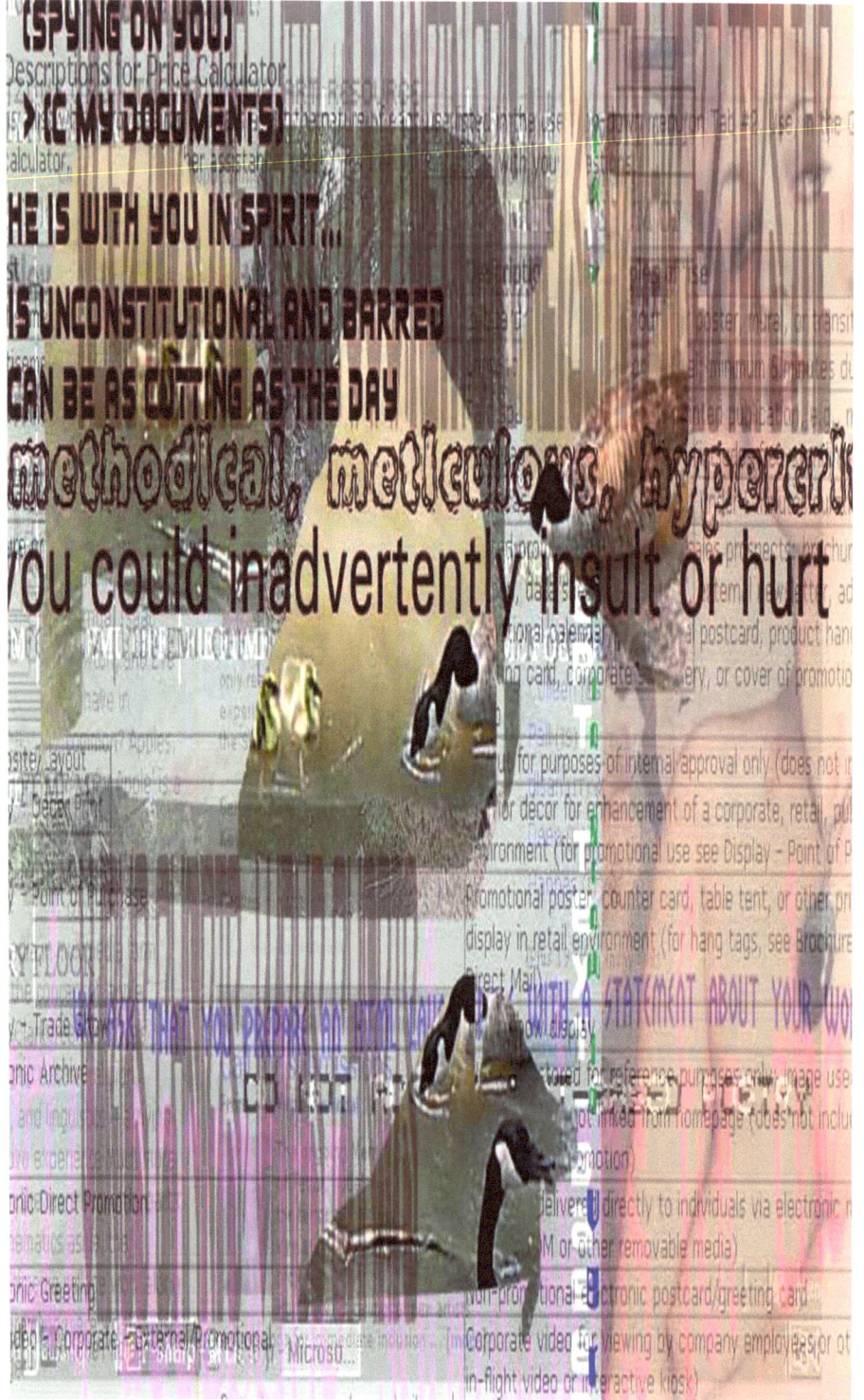

Lewis LaCook "*Klez Tops*"

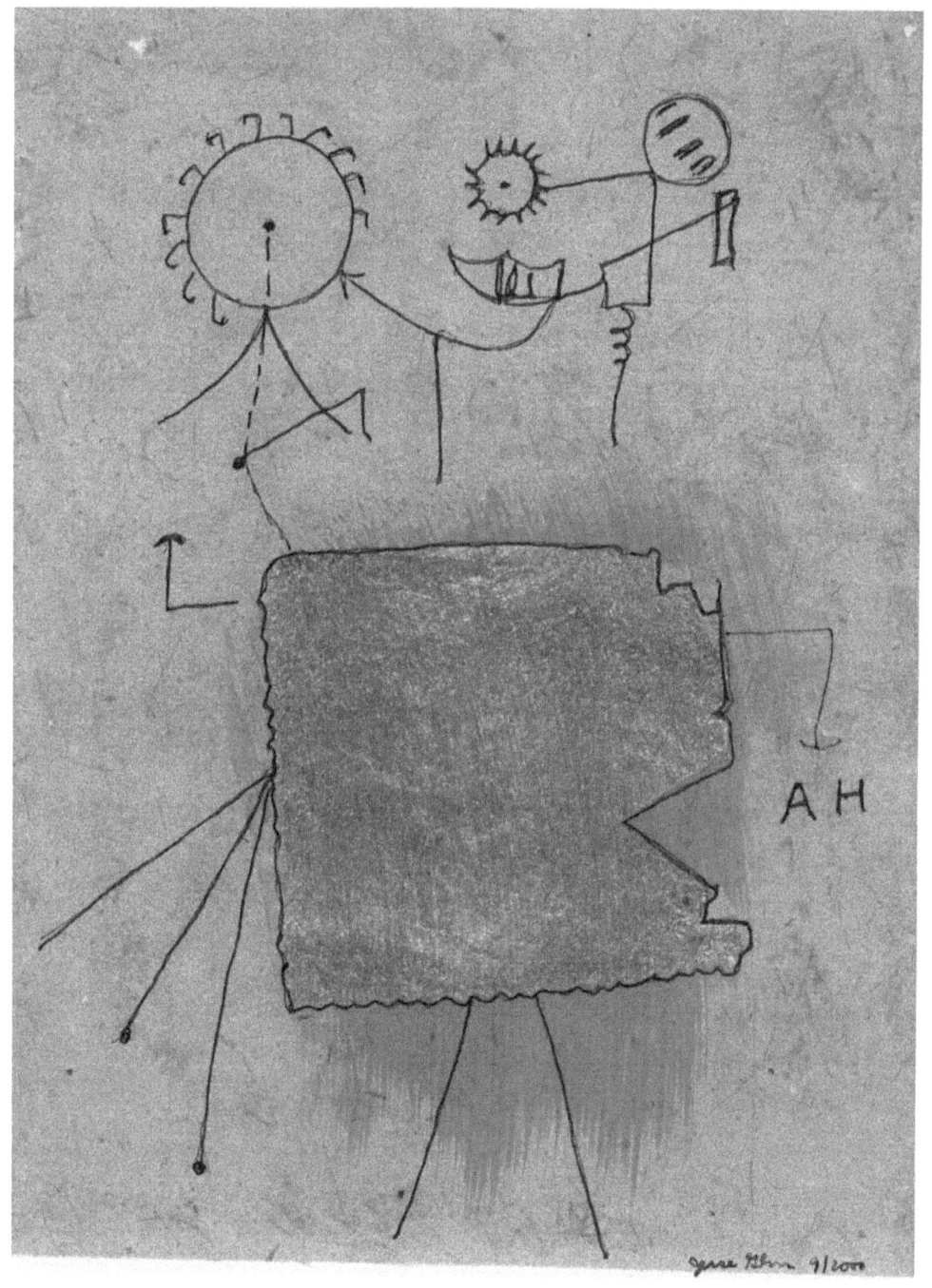

Jesse Glass "*Hell Money Commentary (After Dürer) for D. C.*"

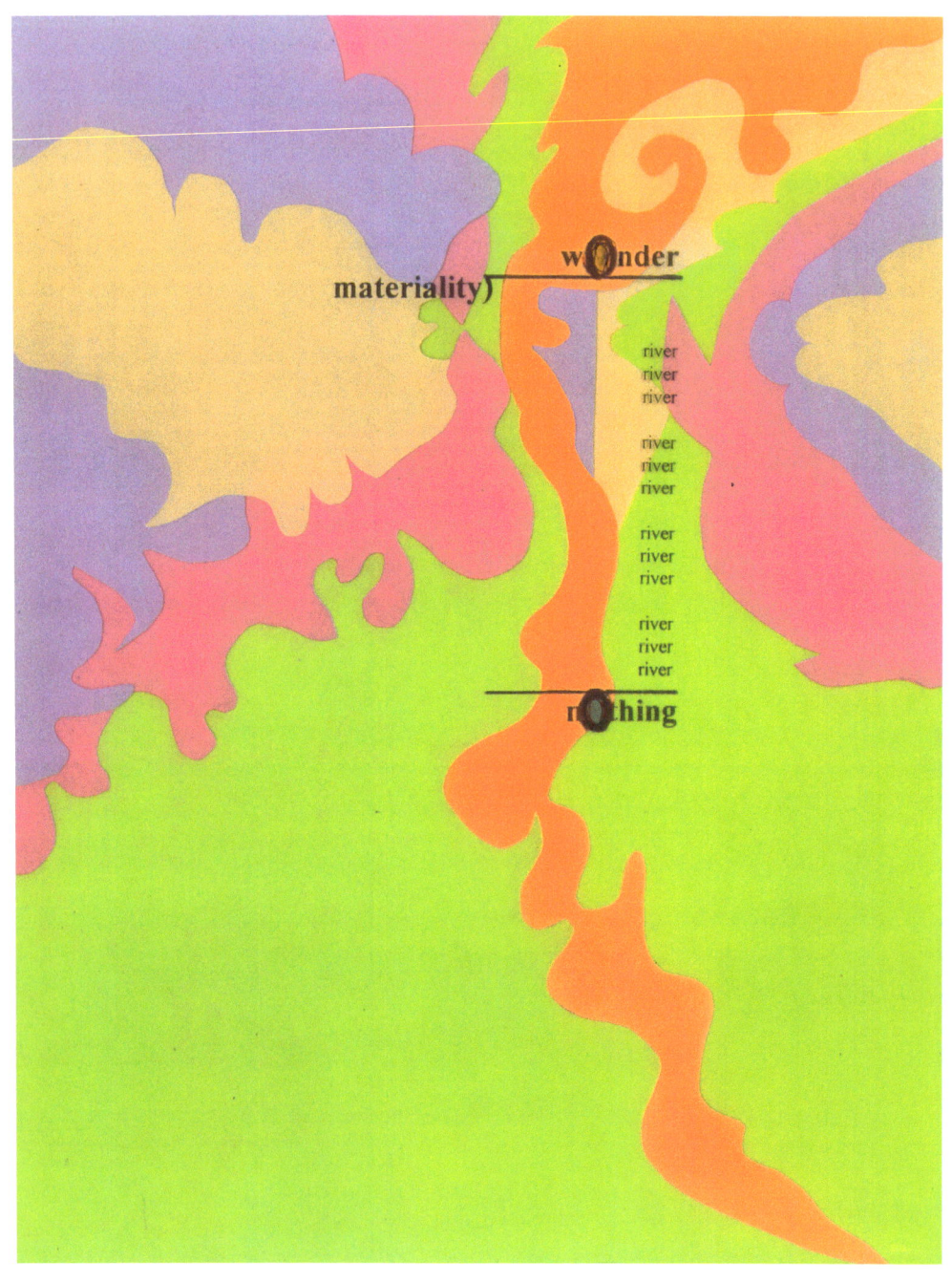

Bob Grumman "*Mathemaku for Robert Lax*"

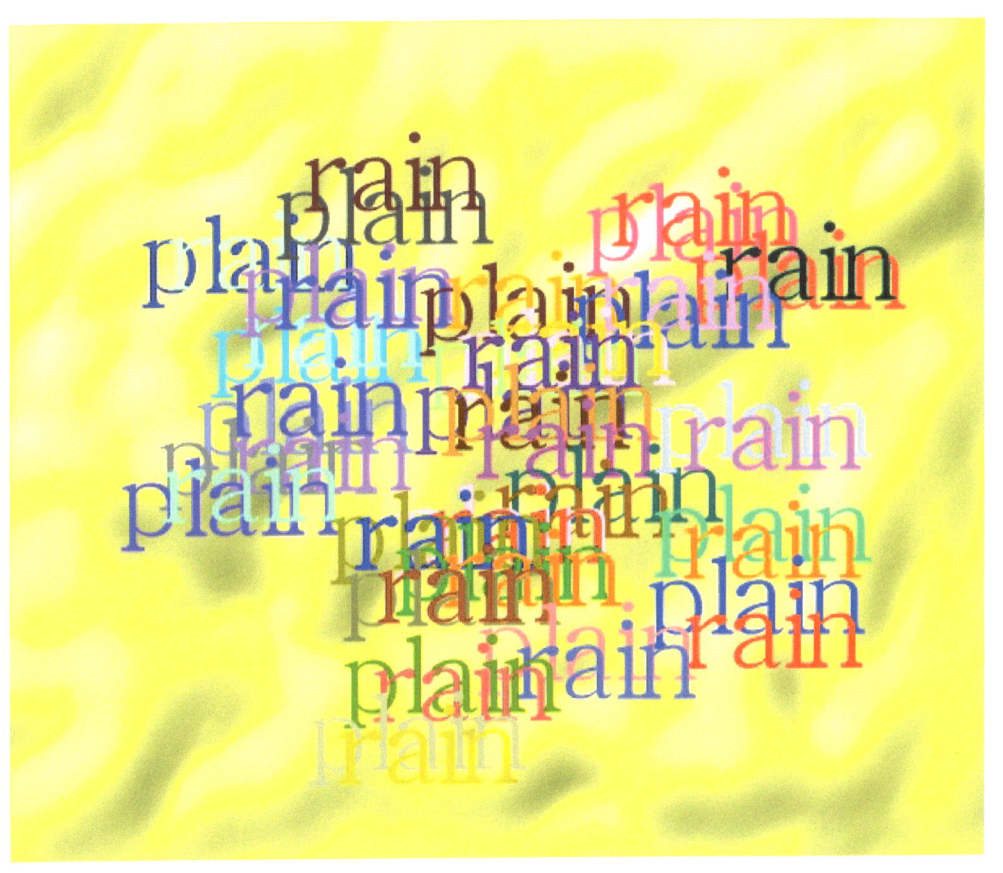

Sheila Murphy "*Plain Rain*"

Second edition printed
December 2008 to
celebrate Xexoxial's
continued commitment
to micro-publishing &
electronic networking.

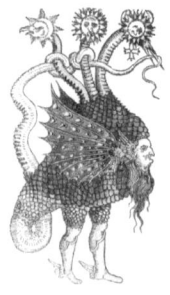

SPIDERTANGLE _the book_ edited by mIEKAL aND
Printed in the Autonomous Republic of Qazingulaza